BEGINNING TO END

# Grass to Milk

by Rachel Grack

BELLWETHER MEDIA • MINNEAPOLIS, MN

Note to Librarians, Teachers, and Parents:

**Blastoff! Readers** are carefully developed by literacy experts and combine standards-based content with developmentally appropriate text.

**Level 1** provides the most support through repetition of high-frequency words, light text, predictable sentence patterns, and strong visual support.

**Level 2** offers early readers a bit more challenge through varied simple sentences, increased text load, and less repetition of high-frequency words.

**Level 3** advances early-fluent readers toward fluency through increased text and concept load, less reliance on visuals, longer sentences, and more literary language.

**Level 4** builds reading stamina by providing more text per page, increased use of punctuation, greater variation in sentence patterns, and increasingly challenging vocabulary.

**Level 5** encourages children to move from "learning to read" to "reading to learn" by providing even more text, varied writing styles, and less familiar topics.

Whichever book is right for your reader, Blastoff! Readers are the perfect books to build confidence and encourage a love of reading that will last a lifetime!

This edition first published in 2020 by Bellwether Media, Inc.

No part of this publication may be reproduced in whole or in part without written permission of the publisher. For information regarding permission, write to Bellwether Media, Inc., Attention: Permissions Department, 6012 Blue Circle Drive, Minnetonka, MN 55343.

Library of Congress Cataloging-in-Publication Data

LC record for Grass to Milk available at https://lccn.loc.gov/2019026685

Text copyright © 2020 by Bellwether Media, Inc. BLASTOFF! READERS and associated logos are trademarks and/or registered trademarks of Bellwether Media, Inc.

Editor: Rebecca Sabelko     Designer: Laura Sowers

Printed in the United States of America, North Mankato, MN.

# Table of Contents

Did you know the **nutrients** in grass become milk?

# Where Is the Most Milk Made?

The European Union produces around 171 tons (155 metric tons) of milk each year.

Mother cows produce milk. But they cannot make it without eating grass. Milk begins in the **pasture**!

Cows are **ruminants**. These animals have four stomachs!

Each stomach does
a special job
to **digest** grass.

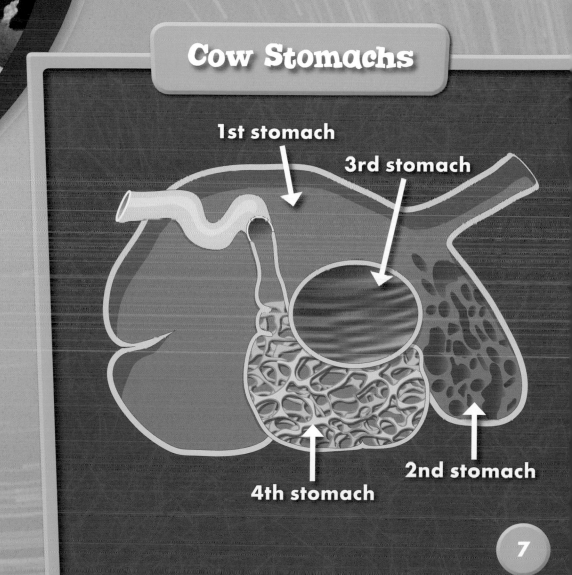

Cow Stomachs

1st stomach

3rd stomach

2nd stomach

4th stomach

The **process** starts when cows **graze**. Cows swallow grass half chewed.

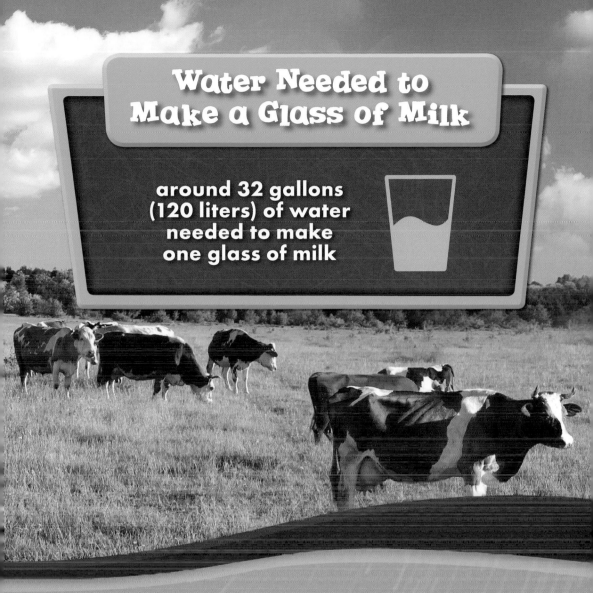

## Water Needed to Make a Glass of Milk

around 32 gallons (120 liters) of water needed to make one glass of milk

Their first two stomachs soften and break down the grass. It becomes **cud**.

Cows throw up and chew the cud. Then they swallow it again.

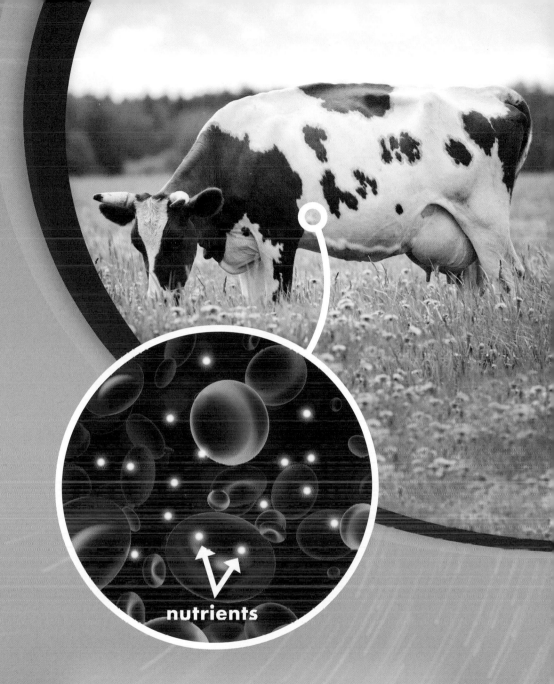

nutrients

Nutrients enter the blood
as the cud is digested.

Blood carries the nutrients to the **udder**. The udder's **mammary glands** use the nutrients to make milk.

Soon the cow is ready
to be milked!

# Factory to Store

milk machine

Dairy farmers milk cows two times a day. The **teats** are hooked up to milk machines.

milk machine

vat

pasteurizer

Milk gets stored and cooled in **vats**.

Milk trucks stop at
dairy farms every day
or two.

Then they take the milk to a factory. It is **pasteurized**.

pasteurizer

Machines bottle the milk.
A date is added to show how
long the milk will stay fresh.
The milk goes to grocery stores.
People buy it to enjoy!

# Grass to Milk

**1** cows digest grass and make milk

**2** cows are milked

**3** milk goes to the factory

**4** milk is pasteurized and bottled

**5** milk goes to grocery stores

There are different types of milk. Some people like creamy whole milk. Others enjoy low-fat milk.

Which kind do you drink?
Cheers!

# Glossary

**cud**—small balls of grass that are not fully digested; cows throw up and chew cud.

**digest**—to break down food

**graze**—to eat grass in a field

**mammary glands**—organs that make milk

**nutrients**—substances needed by people, animals, and plants to stay strong and healthy

**pasteurized**—heated and cooled to keep milk fresh longer

**pasture**—a grassy field

**process**—a number of steps taken to reach an end result

**ruminants**—animals with four stomachs

**teats**—the nipples of a cow; milk comes out of a cow's teats.

**udder**—the bag-like part of a female cow where milk is made

**vats**—large tanks used for storing liquids; vats are used on dairy farms to store milk.

# To Learn More

## AT THE LIBRARY

Carraway, Rose. *Cows on the Farm.* New York, N.Y.:
Gareth Stevens Pub., 2013.

Heos, Bridget. *From Milk to Ice Cream.* Mankato,
Minn.: Amicus, 2018.

Taus-Bolstad, Stacy. *From Grass to Milk.* Minneapolis,
Minn.: Lerner Publications, 2013.

## ON THE WEB

# FACTSURFER

Factsurfer.com gives you
a safe, fun way to find
more information.

1. Go to www.factsurfer.com.

2. Enter "grass to milk" into the search box
   and click Q.

3. Select your book cover to see a list
   of related web sites.

# Index